COASTAL LIVING®
beach house
style
designing spaces that bring the beach to you

COASTAL LIVING®

beach house style

designing spaces that bring the beach to you

Oxmoor House®

ISBN 13: 978-0-8487-3364-3
ISBN 10: 0-8487-3364-9
Library of Congress Control Number: 2009937186

Printed in the United States of America
First Printing 2010

OXMOOR HOUSE

VP, Publishing Director: **Jim Childs**
Editorial Director: **Susan Payne Dobbs**
Brand Manager: **Terri Laschober Robertson**
Senior Editor: **Rebecca Brennan**
Managing Editor: **Laurie S. Herr**

To order additional
publications, call
1-800-765-6400
or
1-800-491-0551.

For more books to
enrich your life, visit
oxmoorhouse.com

COASTAL LIVING® BEACH HOUSE STYLE

Editor: **Katherine Cobbs**
Project Editors: **Emily Chappell, Diane Rose**
Production Manager: **Theresa Beste-Farley**

CONTRIBUTORS

Designer: **Carol O. Loria**
Copy Editor: **Catherine C. Fowler**
Proofreader: **Lauren Brooks**
Indexer: **Mary Ann Laurens**
Interns: **Allison Sperando, Caitlin Watzke**

COASTAL LIVING

Design Director: **Jennifer D. Madara**
Managing Editor: **Amy Lowe Mitchell**
Style Director: **Heather Chadduck**
Senior Editor, Food: **Julia Rutland**
Design Editor: **Steele Thomas Marcoux**
Travel Editor: **Jacquelyne Froeber**
Assistant Features Editor: **Sarah Latta**
Assistant Market Editor: **Bradley Nesbitt**

ART

Senior Designer: **Tempy Segrest**
Designer: **Claire Cormany**
Assistant Photo Editor: **Kristen Shelton Fielder**

COPY

Copy Chief: **Katie Finley**
Copy Editor: **Stephanie Gibson**

PRODUCTION

Production Manager: **Holly H. Goff**
Web/Production Associate: **Kelly Brown Tomas**

EDITORIAL SUPPORT

Office Manager: **Mamie Walling**
Intern: **Brett Bralley**

EDITORS AT LARGE

Melissa Feldman (New York)
David Hanson (Seattle)
Susan Heeger (Los Angeles)
Molly Power Pastor (Atlanta)

CONTRIBUTING EDITORS

Melissa Bigner, Jeff Book, Carolynn Carreño, Beaty Coleman, Audrey Davidow, Susan Stiles Dowell, Marion Laffey Fox, Lucinda Hahn, Char Hatch Langos, Frances MacDougall, Steve Millburg, Alison Miller, Jill Scott Urban

LIFESTYLE GROUP

Managing Editor: **Bill Shapiro**

intro

There's a universal appeal to beach house interiors—they embody a lifestyle that's all about kicking back, living with nature, and focusing on the view. In *Beach House Style*, the editors of *Coastal Living* help do-it-yourselfers bring that look home, whether home is the beach, city, or suburbs.

IN FIND YOUR STYLE you'll see how each coastal region has its own distinct look influenced by climate, culture, and topography. From New England to the Pacific Northwest, this book explores six distinctive coastal styles and offers ideas, color palettes, and insights into what makes the rooms successful.

THE WHAT MAKES A ROOM chapter distills interiors down to their essence, highlighting the key "elements of style" that you can employ to get a similar look in your own home. From lighting and accessories to rugs and textiles, *Coastal Living Beach House Style* will help you make design choices with confidence.

p. 10

contents

introduction 5

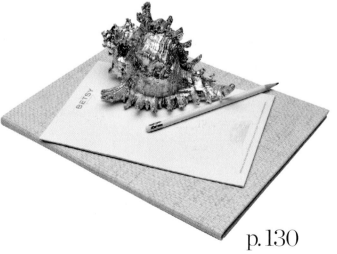

p. 130

p. 84

p. 184

FIND YOUR STYLE

Coastal Living magazine features houses throughout the United States, so we are familiar with the cedar shingles of New England, the pops of pretty color that mark the South all the way down to Key West, the surfer chic of California, and the rugged nature of houses of the Pacific Northwest. It's important to know the iconic signatures of an area, to break old rules, make new ones, and have fun creating a house that's a reflection of who we are no matter where we live.

at home in...
New England

A popular summer destination for those who have weathered the harsh winter climate, the North Atlantic Coast has a storied tradition going back a century that has shaped the unique architectural and interior design style of the region. Summers get hot here, and to thrive in this environment requires a certain hardiness that is reflected in the design.

With no overhead cabinets and open shelving below, the kitchen is easy to navigate. Subway tile on the walls and ceramic tile on the floor keep the space mostly white.

Homeowners are welcomed by this classic Hamptons cottage, with the cedar shingles and a profusion of hydrangeas blooming on the front lawn. Adirondack chairs are to be expected, but the turquoise painted pieces on the porch lend personality.

signature STYLE

CEDAR-CLAD, GAMBREL-ROOFED HOUSES
A traditional no-nonsense type of architecture that holds up to harsh salty winters and ocean winds, this style of house is still being built today.

SMALLER WINDOWS
Because of rushing winds and turbulent storms, the windows tend to be smaller than those we see in other areas on the coast.

BLUE AND WHITE
The classic palette stems from the stripes and colors of old coastal interiors.

SPARE INTERIORS
As part of that Puritan economy, rooms tend to be practical and simple.

RUSTIC EDGES:
Patina is prized in New England, where salvage shops and antiques shops abound.

BEADED BOARD OR SHIPLAP WALLS
Used in ship and barn building, these types of walls are used most often in high traffic areas like the kitchen or bath, but they are so practical and economical that we frequently see them installed today.

LIVING LOCAL
With such abundant forests nearby, materials are often harvested regionally and then implemented in construction.

LOWER CEILINGS
They keep the heat down and circulating, which is especially important on cool summer evenings.

Slipcovered furniture— it's a coastal must-have. And New England is no different.

"THE 'CHARMING HAMPTONS HOUSE'
IS USUALLY THE SUN-BLEACHED,
CEDAR SHINGLE-STYLE HOME WITH
TIMELESS WHITE TRIM, PUNCTUATED
WITH DORMERS AND SHUTTERS."
—JOHN BJORNEN, DESIGNER

A vaulted ceiling visually enlarges a master bedroom. Walls and a ceiling clad in tongue-and-groove cedar contributes to a sense of rustic simplicity.

TAKE IT HOME

THIS PAGE: Floors tend to be bare, with wide, wood planks. If there is a rug, it covers an area rather than the whole floor. Whether the décor is traditional or modern, the spaces are clear of clutter and feel airy and fresh.

1 A striped blue and white rug, soft blue coverlet, and vintage signs and posters decorate a boy's room with a no-nonsense, area-specific approach.

2 This dining room is an unexpected surprise in Penobscot Bay Maine, until you learn that Sister Parish lived and decorated here. The rug inspired the room's bright palette, but the design channels the aesthetics of the legendary decorator.

3 Classic white walls are accented with blues and greens to lend this room a pop of color.

4 In a Maine summer house, the daybed's worn paint says 'no-frills getaway.' But the serenity of the space—with its white walls and painted trunk—conveys luxury, particularly in light of the view through the undressed window.

at home in...

the South

Decades ago, coastal Southern homes were rarely built directly on the beach. It was too hot and too dangerous—tropical storms are nothing new. Instead, they were tucked in among trees and built to take advantage of breezes.

With the emergence of air conditioning, beachfront homes could move out of the shade. Today we see them at the water's edge, fortified, and built on stilts with wraparound porches, fans and grand windows, colors of the sea and sky, and an adherence to tradition—but with a thermostat close at hand.

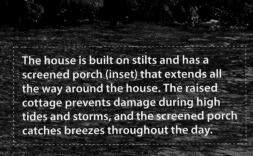

The house is built on stilts and has a screened porch (inset) that extends all the way around the house. The raised cottage prevents damage during high tides and storms, and the screened porch catches breezes throughout the day.

17

"THE BEST SOUTHERN HOUSES HAVE WRAPAROUND PORCHES AND ENOUGH SPACE ON THEIR LOTS FOR BREEZES TO COME IN AND COOL EVERYTHING OFF. THEY HAVE GARDENS AND COLORS INSIDE THE HOUSES THAT REFLECT WHAT YOU SEE OUTSIDE. I LIKE THOSE SEAGLASS COLORS OF BLUE AND GREEN THAT ARE SOFT AND WORN."

—PHILLIP SIDES, DESIGNER

A little Georgian with a few decorative touches, the house has two stories of porches for taking in the view.

Inspired by the sea oats and ocean, pops of fresh and unexpected color give a room full of upholstered furniture vitality.

signature STYLE

NEW URBANISM
The development at Seaside, Florida, with its Victorian and Colonial cottages, inspired miles of beach to become planned beachside villages.

SMALL LOTS
In developments, the lots tend to be small to maximize the feeling of community.

BIG WINDOWS
While air conditioning does most of the cooling these days, big windows are still a welcome feature as they let in great light.

COLOR
Lilly Pulitzer touched the whole summer-loving world, but nowhere more profoundly than in the South, where her punchy lemon/ limeade colors make us feel as happy as they look.

UPHOLSTERED FURNITURE
Again, thanks to air conditioning, the worry of perspiration ruining a silk sofa is gone. And the South is all about welcome, so sink into the cushioned sofas and relax.

SCREENED PORCHES AND SUNROOMS
Screened porches with fans overhead have always been popular, but sunrooms also appear often in the South.

LUSH VEGETATION
Whether it's marsh grasses or tall trees, the heat and humidity of the South are dream conditions for plants.

A LITTLE FORMALITY
Southerners love laid-back luxury, but also favor antiques, which formalize an interior while giving it character.

TAKE IT HOME

THIS PAGE: Fiber cement plank siding that resembles wood covers a three-story Victorian-style house with great water views.

1 Painted rattan furniture adds a feeling of age and character that's also picked up in the brick fireplace.

2 Bold pewter-and-orange Ultrasuede® cushions on Parisian flea-market chairs make for a pleasant juxtaposition of old and new. Alternating stripes give the almost-indestructible seat covers even more punch.

3 A buttery shade on the walls and cabinets bring in the sun-shine. Lower cabinets with inset panels and carved feet instead of baseboards give this new small kitchen a historic feel.

4 "Summertime and the livin' is easy," as they say, and no place is more relaxing than a Southern porch in summer, especially this one, outfitted with a swinging daybed.

1

2

3

4

A wraparound porch, metal roof, and blue shutters are all hallmarks of a classic Key West property, but it's a new house. Even though it's spacious with a second story and dormers, it does not sit large on its property.

at home in...
Key West

O ff the coast of Florida, the climate is hot and tropical, the houses charming and small, and the people who come here as interesting as the place itself. It is known for its city center and festivals, Ernest Hemingway, and hurricanes. And there are the famous feral cats and gypsy chickens that wander the streets, all adding to the eccentricity of the area. Key West style involves a love of the charming and the idiosyncratic, with an appreciation for color—local and literal.

Rattan chairs surround a glass dining table that disappears in deference to the lush vegetation visible through the open doors and transoms.

signature STYLE

CONCH HOUSE
These are houses that sit atop pillars with a wraparound porch, feature louvered shutters, and have pitched roofs with dormers. Burned conch shells were used to make the mortar in the house's construction, hence the name.

METAL ROOF
They deflect the sun and are a practical, if expensive, choice.

VICTORIAN COTTAGE
They're charming and small, wood-shingled with gingerbread details and wraparound porches.

LATIN COLORS
Cuban influences, the area's 1950s aesthetic, and tropical fruit and flowers all make for a flamboyant color palette, including turquoise, aqua, yellow, and coral.

FANS AND AIR-CONDITIONING
Preferred above overhead pendant lighting, fans promote cooling cross breezes.

HEART PINE
A dense wood used in house construction, it's rare and difficult to find, so it is often reclaimed from other sites. Though not termite resistant, it is strong.

POOLS
Pools are commonplace in this balmy climate. The small square footage of the lots mean that most are diminutive plunge pools.

The interiors of this 1890s Victorian cottage have a modern edge—the Eames chair, the vintage counter stools in the kitchen—but it's details like the Dade County pine floors (which are termite resistant) and eccentric collections of art that make it Key West.

"TRADITIONALLY, HOMES IN THE TROPICS HAVE BLUE CEILINGS TO GIVE THE ILLUSION OF SKY AND TO DETER BEES AND HORNETS. YOU CAN SIT ON THE SOFA AND FEEL LIKE YOU'RE OUTSIDE."

—SUZANNE BROWN, DESIGNER

Tight spaces call for a thoughtful design plan. Shelves take advantage of upper cabinet real estate while a counter does double duty as desk and dining surface.

TAKE IT HOME

THIS PAGE: The 1890s Victorian house has gingerbread detailing that makes it appropriate to Key West and its period of origin. A canopy of palms and borders of lush vegetation shade the exterior of the house from the intense sunshine.

1 In this original Conch cottage, a large covered porch allows guests to relax outside, cooled by fans. Indoor-outdoor living is the norm in Key West. The kitchen window pass-through and wall of exterior curtains blur the lines between interior and exterior spaces.

2 A shell-covered kitchen floored in terra-cotta tile is an inventive approach to living and thinking creatively. The backs and sides of upper shelves are painted coral to highlight a collection of large shells and complement the floor.

at home in...
the Caribbean

It's hot and humid here, but breezes are cooling and doors and windows open to promote a true indoor-outdoor communion. The older houses in this area have Western European influences, but more modern structures are totally reflective of the environment. With clear blue seas that deepen in hue the farther out you go, terra-cotta tile covering floors, and stucco walls, the color palette is inspired by the water first and foremost, and then the sand, stone, and vegetation.

Terra-cotta tile roofs over white stucco walls stand out amid the mountainous islands scattered in the distance.

White upholstery recalls the white stucco exteriors and bring a crisp resort chic to the arrangement.

signature STYLE

HIGHLY CARVED, MAHOGANY ANTIQUES
For centuries, Europe's finest mahogany was exported from these islands. A tradition of expressive carving and dense wood furniture can be seen in indigenous pieces.

STONE FLOORING
It's the most practical surface in homes with areas open to the elements.

NO AIR CONDITIONING
Cross breezes travel from one side of the house to the other. In the finest and grandest homes, there is rarely air conditioning with a preference for nature taking precedence.

TROPICAL
Gardens are lush—hot days, heavy rains, cooler nights—and everything seems to grow with abandon.

TILE THATCHED ROOFS
Seen over the trees, scattered tile and thatched roofs tell you that what seems like a deserted island is actually populated.

MOSQUITO NETS
They cover every bed and have become a part of the iconic imagery.

Carved mahogany twin beds are dressed in white linens and protected by mosquito nets that are necessities when you leave doors wide open to the elements. Simple furniture with great patina—the ladder back chairs, the small bedside table—are examples of typical island furniture.

"CONTRAST IS KEY, SO IF THERE IS LIGHT OR WHITE UPHOLSTERY, GROUND IT WITH A COLOR ON THE WALLS AND SNAPPY STRIPED CARPET. LIKEWISE, IF THE UPHOLSTERY IS PATTERNED AND BUSY, KEEP THE CARPET SIMPLE— THINK SISAL OR A SIMPLE DHURRIE."

—MEG BRAFF, DESIGNER

Landscaped into the hill, the metal roofed house keeps doors open to the garden and ocean beyond.

TAKE IT HOME

THIS PAGE: A thatched roof and contrasts of terra-cotta and crisp white seem directly inspired by the landscape. The minimal arrangement keeps the space open and breezy.

1 A cane settee, something you see often in the Caribbean, serves as seating at a long table. The grouping is softly shaded to keep things comfortable under the bright sun.

2 The dining area is covered with plantation shutters that diffuse light yet maintain an airy feel.

3 Built in the 1800s, the cottage was once the great house on a working plantation. European influences are evident with the hipped roof and gingerbread trim, but it is also pure Jamaica, with the stone path and grand staircase leading up to the house.

at home in...
Southern California

Kid-focused—with a pool just beyond the living area—this wood-shingled cottage is landscaped with a thick carpet of green grass and other elements of outdoor diversions.

Part Hollywood hot spot, surfer central, Spanish outpost, and style mecca—it's a little difficult to pinpoint a precise recipe for Southern California style. While the design influences are diverse, it's the climate that makes the style unique. Regular breezes from the Pacific Ocean create a kind environment; the windows here are large and the gardens lush. There are virtually no bugs, so people live outside year-round.

An outdoor living room, with fans hung to push the air around, makes it easy to live outside all year round.

"CALIFORNIA IS ALL ABOUT BEING NATURAL, ORGANIC. THE COLORS ARE CREAMY. I THINK OF MICHAEL TAYLOR'S HOUSES—WITH OVERSTUFFED CREAMY SOFAS AND PLANTS EVERYWHERE, LIKE FICUS TREES. IT STILL LOOKS GOOD TODAY."

—TIM CLARKE, DESIGNER

A modern metal-roofed house with stucco walls is surrounded by palm trees and pots of native California species— rosemary, lavender, and bougainvillea.

A passion for rattan and surfing—they come together where warm woods and soft shades of yellow mix with coastal blue and white prints.

signature STYLE

ECO SAVVY
California was the first to jump on the environmental bandwagon, and, like most of the West, it leads the way in thinking about how to build responsibly.

SUN-KISSED CASUAL
The area is bathed in the colors of a soft sun, with ochers and other yellows that warm (rather than heat) a space.

OPEN TO THE OUTDOORS
There are few bugs, and the air is dry, so living with the doors open all the time is natural.

MIDCENTURY MODERN
1950s and 60s furniture make a statement and give the room a hip feel that seems utterly California.

A LITTLE ARTS AND CRAFTS, A LITTLE CAPE COD
Settled in the early 20th century during the heyday of Arts and Crafts design, that style is naturally popular. Because of the Easterners that have relocated to the West, Cape Cod influences have become common as well.

SPANISH ACCENTS
Mexico is nearby, and there is an abundance of Spanish Colonial design with stucco houses featuring tile roofs and wrought-iron fences.

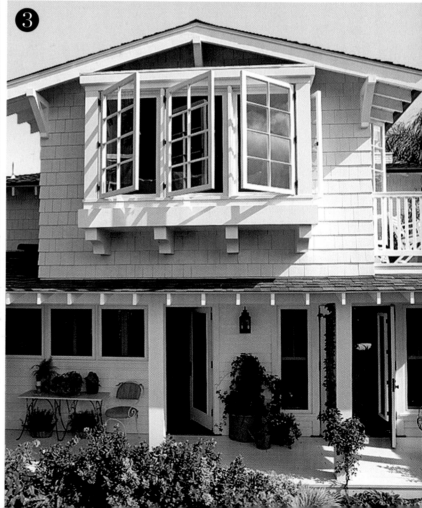

TAKE IT HOME

THIS PAGE: An ergonomically designed banquette surrounds a custom-made ship's table and takes casual dining to a whole other level.

1 Light streams in through windows, but the creamy whites diffuse the glare. Warm wood tones of the mirror and coffee table keep the colors soft.

2 The Arts and Crafts style inspired this house, but it was updated with more windows and a sense of openness.

3 This newly-constructed surf "shack" features windows and doors that are frequently open to keep the transition from indoors to out seamless.

An environmentally savvy house was built with rock walls, branching wood columns, and a sod roof.

at home in...
the Pacific Northwest

With drizzling rain and overcast skies for much of the year, the Pacific Northwest may be the home of Eddie Bauer and Microsoft, but it is also an environmentally conscious region that leads the country in finding ways to preserve the landscape. It's got a rugged sensibility that involves walks and swims in rain when others might wait for sun; bike trips for groceries when others might pull out the SUV; and, when remodeling or constructing a house, working with the land when others would rather work around it.

A great room with kitchen, dining, and living areas has a ladder that leads to a home office and play space upstairs. Made from local woods, the room is all about the landscape.

41

"IT FEELS SO OUTDOORSY IN THE PACIFIC NORTHWEST. IT RAINS OR DRIZZLES AND EVERYONE STILL GOES OUT, GOES ON ABOUT THE DAY. AND THAT RAIN MAKES THE PALETTE THERE DARKER. DARKER COLORS LOOK GOOD, WHERE THEY WOULDN'T WORK IN OTHER AREAS. SO MUCH COMES DOWN TO LIGHT."

—TIM CLARKE, DESIGNER

The paved area stretches the length of the house on the ocean side, making it an ideal spot for watching the surf or kids' tricycle races.

The architectural style of the Pacific Northwest is historically Arts and Crafts, but the tradition of environmentally respectful new construction means that there are a host of new, modern, and eco-friendly houses dotting the landscape.

signature STYLE

ARTS AND CRAFTS STYLE
The area was settled in the 20th Century, and the older houses usually date to that period.

LOCAL MATERIALS
Construction materials often include red cedar, fir beams for architectural trusses, and locally-quarried stone for large fireplaces.

CLERESTORY WINDOWS
Windows that rise above adjacent rooflines maximize light in an often overcast climate.

RUGGED DETAILS
This region has many similarities to New England style houses, but with more rustic detailing.

ECO-MINDED
Cities like Portland, Eugene, and Seattle regularly stand out for their commitment to environmentalism and recycling.

MULTI-CULTURAL INFLUENCES
Arising out of the area's Native American heritage, the region boasts a respect for the environment and a Japanese Zen approach to design.

TAKE IT HOME

THIS PAGE: A boathouse becomes a second cottage for a Washington family. Using wood from their property and a little ingenuity, the cottage nestles into the landscape and serves as a getaway from the getaway.

1 Cleverly tucked under an open staircase, a built-in daybed with bookshelves makes a good spot to read or take a nap.

2 A floor to ceiling stone fireplace made from local material warms up a tall ceilinged room on cool nights and foggy days.

1

2

WHAT MAKES A ROOM?

There are a multitude of elements that make a room special. A chandelier, perhaps. Sparkling glass tiles on a backsplash. Or a great pattern on a chair or pillow. To infuse a room with beach house style, look to natural materials, sun-faded or tropical hues, and classic finishes. Nothing should be too precious. An eclectic mix of loved, lived-in pieces is what beach chic is all about.

living rooms

The mandate for a living room in a beach house is subjective. Sure, white slipcovers, blue and white accents, collections of shells, and nautical relics are all signatures of classic seaside style. But the living rooms we've selected go beyond these characteristics and present a wide range of decorating ideas and color palettes. Whether they offer a cozy nook to kick back with your favorite beach read, a spot to play games with your family, an escape to take a nap, or a cushy sofa to watch movies, they all have a couple of things in common— they're the best spot in the house to relax and catch up on good conversation and undoubtedly the favored alternative to sitting outside.

tailored coordinates

Smooth finishes and crisp fabrics in combination with natural textures and aged woods lend the feeling of a room created over a time.

PATTERNED FABRIC

The soft shades of the blue and white pattern on the chairs and pillows echo the colors of sand and ocean.

THOUGHTFUL STRIPES

The striped rug underfoot, the pleated oval ottoman, and the overstuffed lumbar pillows all add to the nautical feel of the space that seems to be whispering its presence.

GOSSAMER CURTAINS

Sheer window treatments frame the view without interrupting it and allow in the flood of light that keeps the room airy and bright.

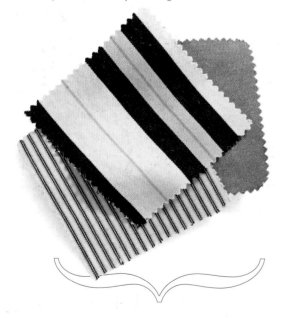

DESIGNER TIP
The semicircular clerestory window overhead echoes the soft shape of the furniture below and keeps the room well lit.

DESIGNER TIP
Cypress walls and rafters in the lofty room give the space warmth that is mediated by the crisp slipcovers and white painted trim.

DESIGNER TIP
Such bold colors work
because of the minimal
foundation pieces:
neutral floor coverings
and window treatments,
lucite nesting tables, and
a clean-lined floor lamp.

DESIGNER TIP
Peachy-coral accents paired with apple-green were inspired by the Sister Parish wallpaper that once hung above the wainscotting.

Sister Parish chic

Bright sherbet hues are refreshingly tropical, but combined with restraint, give this space the perfect dose of beach elegance.

PINK AND GREEN
The house was originally decorated by legendary designer Sister Parish, but time had taken its toll. Still the color palette—the combination of green walls and upholstery and pink pillows—stayed. The colors are fresh and lively and fun, and will never go out of style.

FAMILY FRIENDLY
A naturally woven rug and leather pillows add to the soft durability of the room designed for a young family.

moody hues

Slip-covered seating becomes elegant against saturated, dark walls, providing a cool, crisp escape from the intensity of the day.

DARK PAINT EVERYWHERE

A deep purple-brown color covers walls, trim, and shelving, creating a seamless cocoon that works well in a media room or a library. Light linen slipcovers on the seating infuse the room with a restful airiness.

FABRIC

Combining fabrics that have similar tones but different sizes and types of patterns adds energy and keeps the look from feeling too matchy-matchy.

NAPPING NOOKS

Transform an extra closet into a cozy nap nook with a built-in twin bed, reading sconces, and drapery partitions—perfect after a day at the beach.

In a repurposed closet, a custom-built daybed has ikat running horizontally (called railroaded) to prevent seams. It is upholstered vertically on the skirt.

DESIGNER TIP
Rather than close off nooks or bonus areas with doors, curtains add drama and keep the feel of the room soft.

DESIGNER TIP
A broad Roman shade
made from striped ikat
covers three windows,
keeping the seamlessness
of the room intact.

ECO-CHIC
The sealed, direct-vent (chimney-free) gas fireplace decreases air pollution and increases energy efficiency by preventing heated air from slipping outside.

DESIGNER TIP
In such a large space, a single pendant light might look wimpy. These double pendant lights have gold finishes on the interior that create a warm glow.

eclectic mix

A trio of timeless colors—plum, aqua and coral—are tied together with creams and taupes, keeping this funky gathering space current.

DIVIDED SPACES
Rugs, color, and even tables can help create rooms within rooms in a living space—an attractive idea for large, open floor plans.

ROUGH HEWN
In the rug and the fir plank over the mantel, a rustic texture takes any preciousness out of the space.

PUNCH OF COLOR
A shot of unexpected bold color—the hit of salmon here—connects the stairwell wall color to the upholstery on the club chair.

sixties chic

A rustic, cabin atmosphere is tempered with layers of soft fabric, white painted furniture, and pieces with modern lines.

PUNCHES OF BLUE
Blue borders the Roman shades, a good choice for window treatments to soften the expanse of wood paneling. The upholstery play of blue with white welting and white with blue welting in front of the fireplace is all dictated by the striped carpet.

SHOTS OF CHARTREUSE
In the accessories is ideal interpretation of beach landscape—royal blue waters, white sand, and sea oats.

CADILLAC CHAIRS
The retro vibe starts with the chrome arched arms of the white leather chairs. The low ceilings and vintage outdoor furniture keep the thought alive.

DESIGNER TIP
The contrast between the chrome chairs and the stone fireplace and other woods reaches a cool/comfortable balance.

Jackson Pollock

FOUR SEASON

treehouse tower

Glassed in and perched among the tree-tops, this great room brings the outdoors in. Like a watchtower or lighthouse, the room allows its occupants to take in the view while maintaining privacy naturally.

CANOPY CAMOUFLAGE
This home's minimal footprint doesn't detract from its high style. A wall of windows makes the house feel more treehouse than cottage. Angled vertical supports give a sense of the architecture.

BUILT-IN SOFAS
Visible wood grain on the arms of the fixed seating continues the woodsy style. Upholstery in royal blue with coordinating beige linen adds softness.

TONAL PALETTE
The deep green of the leaves through the windows and the saturated blues in the upholstery strike a serious tone, but the lucite coffee table and the glass walls keep things light.

ECO-CHIC
Angled windows allow for maximum light to enter the room. Glass panels at the base of the windows open like trap doors to allow for breezes and elimi-nate the need for air conditioning.

SUNKEN CENTER
Wide plank high gloss wood floors surround the sunken centerpiece of the room, which is painted with blue and green stripes.

ELEMENTS OF STYLE

PUT THESE ELEMENTS OF A COASTAL LIVING ROOM TOGETHER IN YOUR HOUSE, AND FEEL THE OCEAN BREEZES.

plants

The soothing green of palm fronds and tall grasses suggest a beach aesthetic.

tables

In these rooms, the most successful tables tend to be light, movable, and casual enough to handle a pair of propped feet.

pillows

Solid, patterned, or graced with a nautical motif, pillows add comfort and style.

paint

Creamy whites and seaglass shades are one of the simplest ways to bring coastal style home.

rugs

Seagrass and sisal are the carpets of choice, but you often see dhurries and other casual style rugs.

"TRANSLUCENT LAMP BASES ARE CASUAL, AIRY, AND OH-SO-BEACHY."

glass

Whether it's bowls of beach glass or a ship in a bottle, glass conjures up the sea, especially in bottle green.

upholstery

Deep cushions and blousy slipcovers have a casualness to them that invite sitting back and sinking in, taking in a book or a video, gazing at a view.

LIGHTING
Artificial light from nautical lamps and overhead lights provide a seafaring style.

WINDOW TREATMENTS
We don't see curtains very often, but they are necessities in some rooms for privacy or to block out light at the most intense hours of the day. Sheers work well, diffusing light and softening glares.

dining rooms

At the coast, there are few schedules. Breakfast is when everyone wakes up. Lunch when everyone needs a break. Dinner when everyone is all cleaned up. The most important part is that everyone is together. And what better place to gather than around the table, whether for a casual family meal or set for a more special occasion with guests. Inside or outside, everybody gathers to celebrate the moment…wherever you live.

view gazing

Nothing here can distract from the view. Large plate glass windows offer an unob-structed feast for the eyes. Whether it's a lush backyard, desert landscape, or city skyline, if the view is notable, let it take center stage.

MODERN ICONS
In a sun-drenched room, a Saarinen table surrounded by four Bertoia modern chairs strikes a clean contrast with the wood windows that look out to the ocean in the distance.

BLUE CUSHIONS
The blue linen on the chair cushions repeats the blue of the ocean making a visual connection.

OBJETS D'ART
Binoculars at the ready for taking in the expansive view. A loose arrangement plucked from the grassy expanse outside. A seashell gathered during a walk along the shore. Each adds beauty, functionality, and personality to this welcoming space.

DESIGNER TIP
A pair of oars stand by the door, ready for an outdoor adventure.

DESIGNER TIP
Embroidered, flame-stitch, and botanical prints on pillows are a haphazard combination that works thanks to their shared shades of dusty blue.

breakfast nook

Work space, reading space, eating space, and relaxing retreat, this casual dining corner's overstuffed down cushions provide unexpected comfort for multiple pursuits.

BANQUETTE
Tucked into a corner and layered with colorful patterned pillows, the banquette is an ingenious move in a breakfast room. It maximizes existing space and creates seating for lounging.

MARBLE MARVEL
A slab of green marble is an earthy counterpart to the bamboo table base and the green trim of the window and lattice beyond.

ORGANIC TEXTURE
Worn walnut chairs with woven seats, the patina of aged bamboo, and camel-colored linen upholstery all come together in an Old World, lived-in way.

eclectic mélange

Hats off to this well-orchestrated exercise in eclectic style—traditional, contemporary, rustic, and refined all in one space. Add in bright splashes of color tempered by a neutral background for an engaging effect.

BRASS ACCENTS
Tall candlestick lamps emphasize the height of the space while brass hanging lanterns warm the room.

GRAPHIC RUG
It's large enough to ground the table and chairs, and its almost raspberry color brings out the red accents in the art.

NEW TAKE ON OLD FORM
The dining table is a new piece, but it looks as though it was made from old wood because of its warm patina. The 1970s sideboard and Bertoia chairs give the whole space a contemporary energy.

DESIGNER TIP
This mosaic-like artwork is the jumping off point for masterful color scheme.

a mod mix

Timeworn finishes mixed with clean modern pieces gives this gathering space a fresh, fun look that says, "put your feet up, lean back, and sit and stay awhile."

SANDY GRAY TRIM
The reverse of a more typical paint approach (color on the walls and white for the trim), soft gray-green trimwork frames the views with a hue more in tune with the landscape than bright white.

TABLES WITH PATINA
Made from attractively distressed, reclaimed wood, the coffee and dining tables add just the right amount of beachy texture to the room.

CONTEMPORARY SEATING
Clean lines and the crisp matte finish of the dining chairs make a contemporary statement against the rustic farm table.

BARE WOOD FLOORS
Dining rooms are great places to show off beautiful hardwoods, which are also easier to keep clean than rugs.

"AT THE BEACH, YOU WANT TO SPEND TIME WHERE EVERYONE CAN BE TOGETHER. ONE GIANT ROOM WHERE YOU COOK, EAT, WATCH TV, AND PLAY GAMES JUST WORKS."

—INTERIOR DESIGNER TIM CLARKE

a stately room

A pass-through lessens the formality of this dining area by connecting the cook to the guests. The shelves that separate the spaces are all about displaying loved objects and art.

A NO-FAIL APPROACH
A lantern, chairs, and a rectangular table seem like the tried and true setup. But this one has a few surprises.

RATHER THAN CHAIRS
A pair of painted slipcovered rattan settees pulls up to the 7-foot custom oak table. It makes seating more flexible and intimate if the occasion calls for squeezing in as many guests as possible.

SLIPPER CHAIRS AT THE END
We see them in boudoirs or flanking a fireplace, but these chairs, with no armrests, give some air to the arrangement.

BLUE RUG
It's large enough to hold all the furniture, and it coordinates with both the view and the collections on the shelves.

DESIGNER TIP
This oversized lantern is dramatic but works with the scale of the room.

DESIGNER TIP
The x-pattern on the chair backs mimics the lower window frames.

easy living on the porch

Nothing could be easier than a lazy afternoon spent on a covered patio. The roof provides shade from the sun and protection from the elements, while the screens keep bugs at bay when dining alfresco.

RAIL SHELF
A two-by-eight board serves as a cap to the railing of the porch but also can be used as a place to lean or set a drink or a plate when entertaining.

SIMPLY IRON
Four x-back chairs around a small round table make an intimate spot for breakfast or dinner. Lumbar pillows soften the metal seatbacks.

A COOL CONCRETE FLOOR
The plain stained floor can withstand whatever Mother Nature dishes out and can be hosed off as needed.

open concept

The open kitchen has perhaps surpassed the great room as the feature most desired in homes nowadays. It facilitates connection with family and guests and keeps the cook from feeling like an exile.

GREAT ROOM
Located between the kitchen and living area, the dining area is a classic arrangement—rectangular table, upholstered chairs, center runner, and candles suggest that this a dining table and not a catchall surface.

HANGING FIXTURE
The large pendant light illuminates the meal, yet its size and varied finish distinguish it from the pendants hanging over the counter.

COORDINATED COLORS
The table is light, new wood and contrasts with the reclaimed wood on the floor. The coral color chosen for the dining chairs connects with the more opaque pumpkin cushions in the living area.

DESIGNER TIP
The rectangle table echoes the shape of the kitchen island.

ELEMENTS OF STYLE

PUT THESE DISPARATE ELEMENTS TOGETHER AND YOU'LL HAVE A GREAT LOOKING COASTAL DINING SPACE.

mix and match chairs

Use what you have but tie it together with matching fabric or paint.

glass accessories

Reflective like the sea, mercury glass, mirrors, and opalescent pieces add shimmer and shine.

colorful prints

Like frosting on a cake, a few well chosen patterns take a room from ho hum to holy cow!

beachy centerpieces

A glass bowl of seashells. A crab trap full of autumn gourds. Display found objects in unique ways with a beachy bent.

natural texture

Burlap, linen, raw silk, and slubby cotton are all durable fabrics that go well with anything and stand the test of time.

organic shapes

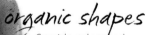

Seaside colors and free-form shapes are casual by nature and perfect for beach house style.

painted furniture

Need more storage, but don't like the sideboard you inherited from Aunt Ethel? Just paint it!

DESIGNER TIP
Chandeliers make rare appearances in coastal homes, and when you do see them they are often encrusted with seashells or colored beads, as is the case here.

kitchens

You can almost write a recipe for the ultimate coastal kitchen—a dash of sea glass or ocean-inspired tiles, a heap of open space, ample doses of white, aqua blue, or sunny shades, all centered on an island for serving and gathering. Counter stools, open shelves, pendant lights to illuminate, and streamlined appliances are like garnishes to finish the dish. Coastal kitchens are practical yet stylish, and just like every home, the center of it all.

50s diner

This kitchen exudes happiness. The shine of chrome and homespun accessories like the blue-tinted mason jars, enameled pot on the stove, and jadeite dishes on the counter and in cabinets keep the midcentury vibe going.

RETRO APPLIANCES
They're brand new, but the aqua color and vintage look make them feel like refurbished discoveries from a junk/treasure shop.

CLASSIC LIGHT FIXTURES
Lighting that's in sync with the period of the space lends authenticity to the design.

PATCHWORK TILE
The backsplash, which reaches the bottom of the overhead cabinet, combines different sizes of aqua tile applied in a seemingly random pattern. The blue and green mix sets the palette for accessories and dishes.

OVERHEAD CABINETS
Some closed, some open, some glassed in—all three varieties leave room for display and convenient storage.

DINER STOOLS
Simple round cushioned stools don't obstruct the view of the great room and add to the kitchen's vintage flavor.

DESIGNER TIP
Classic schoolhouse pendants are the crowning jewels in this neo-vintage seaside kitchen.

POURED CONCRETE COUNTERTOPS
Concrete counters cover every surface. The island's bar height steps down to counter height to hide dirty dishes from the great room beyond.

DESIGNER TIP
Antique brass
pendants with
milk-glass shades
mimic the lines of
the vent hood
and relate to the
colors in the tile.

tile to the top

Taking the tile all the way up to the ceiling accentuates the height of this small kitchen giving it a feeling of grandeur. Burnished metals give a dose of bling to the mono-chromatic sandy palette.

OCTAGONAL TILES
The star of this kitchen, they cover the whole rear wall. The effect is dramatic—it reads like wallpaper, but the texture and depth of the tiles is captivating.

BRONZE AND BRASS
A simple oil-rubbed bronze hood presides over the stove and sets the color tone on that far wall. Brass hardware at the sink, on the refrigerator, and in the lighting pick up the warm tones.

QUARTZ COUNTERS
It's a man-made material but it looks natural with the ceramic tile wall. The smooth finish is clean and simple against the patterned tile.

NO OVERHEADS
Cabinets are tucked into a sidewall and a closet is used for storage, all to allow for the tiled wall.

SEATING
Backless stools make space for guests to perch while you're preparing a meal.

all hands on deck

Clean, spare, with it all right there, this galley kitchen is all about being part of the action while entertaining. Basic white and natural wood allow for the focus to turn to the food and the view.

SHIPLAP WALLS
The space feels sleek, but the shiplap covered white walls give it a beach-casual feel.

13-FOOT BUTCHER-BLOCK ISLAND
Such a long island creates a division between the kitchen area and the rest of the living area. It also provides extensive carving and prep space.

DIRECTOR'S CHAIRS
The white fabric and wood frames connect with the white cabinet faces and creates a cohesive look for the kitchen space. These bar-height chairs are a fun and comfortable alternative to stools.

DESIGNER TIP
Without the whitewashed paneling and a beaded-board ceiling, this kitchen might be considered "minimalist modern," but these finishes lend a laid-back feeling to this expansive gathering place.

WELL-ANCHORED
Dark, oil-stained plank floors ground the light-filled airy space and lend to its nautical feel.

green day

Soaring cabinets in a daring shade of palm-frond green in combination with shimmering chrome, splashes of red, and sleek black countertops come together in this decidedly modern kitchen.

UNEXPECTED COLOR
Most kitchens are white or maybe yellow, but it's rare to find a green kitchen. The bold shade is tempered a bit with blocks of white and the frosted glass fronts on the cabinet doors.

LETTERED IN STYLE
Upper cabinets often hold things we forget about immediately. Out of sight out of mind. But the letters decorating each make it easy to remember where something that does not get frequent use is stored.

FROSTED GLASS-FRONTED CABINETS
We see more of these today. Open shelves present a challenge because they require order, but frosted glass allows an idea of what is inside but prevents viewers from seeing the real disorder.

STAINLESS STEEL SPLASHES
The metal is a cool counterpoint to the green cabinets. It's carried throughout with industrial stools, hanging light fixtures, and wall-mounted clock.

cool contrast

Soothing in shades of whipped cream and espresso bean, this kitchen boasts strong horizontal lines repeated in the shelving, refrigerator's drawers, island, console, and lantern. The model airplane, converging beams of the ceiling rafters, and the painting all suggest movement.

WRAP-AROUND SHELVING
Open shelving requires order because tableware is exposed, but it is also an invitation to display objects and collections, particularly on the hard-to-reach top row.

DARK WOOD
The contrast of the dark wood countertops with the white walls and island gives the space an ethnic feel supported by the collections.

FAUCET AS SCULPTURE
The enormous faucet presides over the sink and adds interest. Fixtures are sculptural and they can decorate the space as well as provide a function.

SCHOOLHOUSE STOOLS
More pleasant for hanging out than actually sitting and eating a meal on, the stools continue the unadorned industrial vibe.

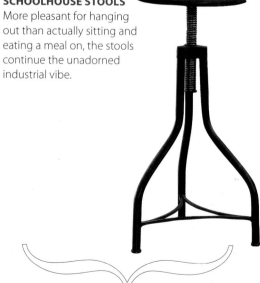

PAINTED BEAMS
Imagine if the V-groove paneling or beams were not painted. The contrasts would be too great. It's much better for them to be solid white and provide some depth without making the eye bounce from dark brown wood to white surfaces.

93

DESIGNER TIP
A scarf as window valance, flowers in a julep cup, and a basket of fruit on the table are feminine accents in a rustic space.

surf shack simplicity

Unfinished wood plank walls, simple shelving and cabinets, and a high-gloss varnished countertop suggest a space lovingly crafted by hand over time. Nothing here is too precious or pretentious.

PERFECTLY PETITE
Proving that great things come in small packages, this pint-sized kitchen keeps all the accoutrements at the cook's fingertips—diminutive range, deep sink, and recessed fridge.

RUSTIC-MEETS-CONTEMPORARY
Balanced splashes of white temper the all-wood kitchen and infuse it with a clean, modern feel.

TABLE AS CENTERPIECE
With the table as focal point, this kitchen is all about gathering to share a meal before heading back to enjoy wide-open spaces.

VINTAGE COPPER
Playing off the wood walls, the copper light fixture's warm patina says "vintage" without screaming "relic!" and is perfectly fitting for a homespun kitchen.

"SALVAGE YARDS ARE LOADED WITH AMAZING CASTAWAYS LIKE ANTIQUE LIGHTS THAT SIMPLY NEED REWIRING."

ELEMENTS OF STYLE

SET THE TONE WITH EYE-CATCHING ACCENTS AND GLISTENING FINISHES. USE POPS OF COLOR THROUGHOUT.

bright appliances

Stainless, white, or black appliances are expected, but choices in color make a bold statement.

comfy barstools

A thick padded seat and backrest make it an easy choice to keep the cook company.

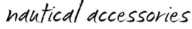

lighting with history

Research the period of your home or favored style and choose lighting that relates.

nautical accessories

Rope handles, shell bowls, and manufactured coral towel hooks are a few ways to bring the beach back home.

seaglass-inspired glassware

Translucent blue and green glass seem born of the sea and sky.

sleek fixtures

Glistening fixtures reflect light and add a bit of bling to a beachy kitchen.

colorful dishware

White dishes have their place, but tableware in cheery colors infuses the kitchen with sunshine.

97

DESIGNER TIP
Unadorned windows with transoms let the light pour in, keeping this kitchen bright even on overcast days.

DESIGNER TIP
A multi-level, U-shaped island is this kitchen's workhorse, offering prep, seating, and storage space. Plus, it has refined cabinetmaker features like the turned leg supports.

bathrooms

The coastal bath is usually an end of the day indulgence, when you wash the salt and the sting of the sun away and put on your new, relaxed self. Attached to master bedrooms, baths tend to be spacious and pampering, with a separate shower and tub. Guest baths may have just a shower, but the space is still a retreat, with views of the water or out to the garden and tile that might bring the colors of the sand, sky, or water inside.

eco-serene

Washed in earthy hues, this spa-like bath has an organic feel with a view that brings the outdoors in.

GLASS WALL

The bath is one large room, but the tub sits before a wall of windows that can be opened to let in breezes. The windows can also go from clear to opaque with the flip of a switch for privacy.

SINK

A partial tile wall separates the tub from the top mount square sink. A pendant light rather than sconce illuminates the space.

TACTILE FLOOR

A pebble floor makes you feel as if you are bathing in nature. It also offers radiant heat, which is much more efficient than baseboard heat or forced air.

DESIGNER TIP
Chocolate subway tile stacked vertically is a masculine, modern touch on a wall designed to create separation in this large space.

101

102

DESIGNER TIP
Traditional lighting and accessories blend seamlessly with the clean lines of the Parsons style vanity.

classically coastal

Salvaged shutters and windows set the tone for this clever master bath that has a timeless feel.

RECLAIMED AND RUSTIC
A pair of old lattice windows gets a new life by replacing the glass with mirrors cut to size. Shutters used as window treatments provide privacy and warmth.

SUBTLY STRIPED
Beaded-board wainscoting pairs with pinstripe wallpaper on the window wall to carry the nautical stripe element throughout the entire room.

FINISHING TOUCHES
A trio of traditional swivel sconces, rather than unflattering overhead fluorescent lighting, illuminates the vanity. The lights' nickel finish coordinates with the old-fashioned sink and bathtub fixtures.

cedar surround

Rich cedar boards are naturally bug and moisture repellent, making them a good choice for damp spaces and closets.

HORIZONTAL BOARDS
Instead of costly tile, cedar boards stand in to create a chic wall-to-wall surround in the bath. The contrast with the white claw-foot tub creates a play between light and dark, old and new.

PENNY TILES
The floor has traditional penny tile, a look that is always attractive.

LIGHTING
A small window/porthole allows in natural light during the day, and ships' lights illuminate the space at night.

DESIGNER TIP
Wood varieties like cedar and teak are water-friendly so no curtain is needed for this shower-tub combo.

DESIGNER TIP
A rain shower head is a sensory treat in this large, refreshingly green shower stall.

DESIGNER TIP
The round rug breaks up the right angles and provides softness underfoot.

palm inspired

The palm frond fabric on the pillows and curtains in the bedroom beyond inspired the tile choice and prove that carrying a theme throughout is impactful.

TILE FLOOR TO CEILING
Colored green tiles fill the walls in this bath, while white tiles cover the shower floor. Large marble tiles were chosen for the rest of the floor.

SHEATHED IN WOOD
A drop in tub fits into a marble surround clad in wood. The ledge is wide enough for seating or lining up shampoo and other necessities. The tub resembles a piece of furniture and coordinates with the wood accents in the neighboring master bedroom.

CLEVER CONSOLE
A long console with a square built-in sink has great storage—drawers, doors (to cover the pipes), and open shelves that allow easy access to rolled-up towels.

DESIGNER TIP
Cream paint, muted hues in the wallpaper, and natural straw shades make for a monochromatic masterpiece.

"I THINK BATHROOMS GOT TOO BIG IN NEW CONSTRUCTION. IT IS REALLY A UTILITY ROOM FOR PERSONAL GROOMING AND SHOULD BE UNCLUTTERED, CLEAN, LIGHT."

—JACKIE TERRELL, DESIGNER

papered
and
pretty

It's true that great things come in small
packages, and this room is no exception.
It is fully functional, loaded with style,
but not over the top.

SCONCE OVERHEAD
Making the most of a small space, an overhead
sconce—rather than a pendant light or a pair
flanking the mirror—casts a soft light over the room.

COW PARSLEY PATTERN
The subtle wallpaper print adds something organic
and interesting to the small space.

MARBLE COUNTER
A marble slab and backsplash with squared edges
covers the counter. Ample space on either side of
the undermount sink accommodates accessories.
The shelf of this limed oak console holds towels.

POCKET PRIVACY
To save room in tight spaces like this one, consider
pocket doors like the one here, which opens to the
plum-colored hallway reflected in the mirror.

DESIGNER TIP
Forget a solid piece of mirrored
glass. The framed mirror here
has presence and elongates
the space.

ELEMENTS OF STYLE

INTRODUCE BEACHY STYLE TO THE BATH WITH THESE PRODUCT PICKS.

industrial lighting

Fixtures like these have a utilitarian feel that works wherever task lighting is needed.

monogrammed towels

It's a classic personal touch that caps off a bathroom.

square mirror

A change of pace from the typical rectangle. Take a mirror tile to the frame shop and create your own masterpiece.

coastal color

Blues tinged with a bit of black have a dusted down, gray quality reminiscent of ocean and sky before a thunderstorm.

seaglass-inspired hardware

Crystal knobs are commonplace in bathrooms, but milk glass versions in beachy hues scream beach chic.

textured tile

Tile with a bit of rustic tooth seems more like stone than a manufactured product. They provide traction on wet floors.

saltwater soap
with rosemary and patchouli
4 oz.

SAIPUA
brooklyn, ny

SAIPUA
brooklyn, ny

nautical accessories

Pretty sea soaps arranged in a large clam shell turned soap dish or a beach tote filled with rolled towels make a bathroom feel like vacation.

neutral wall paint

Walls ranging from cream to café au lait are easy to live with and allow you to change the look of a space by swapping out accessories.

DESIGNER TIP
A repeated small scale fabric mimics the pattern of the tiles on the floor.

DESIGNER TIP
When you stumble upon a great find, snag it. A simple perch was handcrafted and painted for this deep salvaged farm sink.

bedrooms

As much as a coastal house is a gathering place, the master of ceremonies and orchestrator of all the fun needs a little down time too. Most beachside bedrooms are pared down and easy on the eyes, requiring little maintenance and primping. These rooms tend to be soft and neutral, full of pillows and cooled by a fan. Your guests deserve their own haven too, with everything they need close at hand. Guest rooms, by design, are brighter, more efficient spaces. The bed may even be more layered so that the room is a pleasure to look at and a cocoon of comfort.

summer flashback

This home's original cedar-shake style was resurrected with knotty pine beams, walls, ceilings, and floors.

ARCHITECTURAL DETAILS
New pine trim and details on the ceilings and walls replicate the original pine. People rarely do totally wood houses anymore. But this look is reminiscent of the summer houses of half a century ago.

CLASSIC ELEMENTS
Designed to combine the classic look of a luxury liner with a fun, beach-weekend feel, this guest room boasts a place for writing postcards, a swing arm lamp for reading in bed, and a bedside table for resting a book.

FABRICS
Comfortable yet resilient fabrics such as faux leather, terry cloth, wool, and linen on slipcovered furniture, pillows, and window treatments can be switched out seasonally.

STICK TO A SINGLE COLOR
The mood of the beach comes through in the saturated citrus shade that pops against the all-wood backdrop.

DESIGNER TIP
Beachy elements like the starfish and coral lamp keep this room grounded in its seaside location.

DESIGNER TIP
The large wood timber to the left of the bed actually reaches up from the kitchen through the master bedroom floor. It's a great place for hooks that hold robes, raincoats, and other necessities.

grand master

Cathedral ceilings, a bed centered in the middle of the room defined by draped fabric, and a long steamer trunk give this bedroom an elegant, traveler feel.

MOSQUITO NETTING
It adds the drama in the room and, when closed, makes it possible to leave windows wide open at night.

AREA RUGS
The space is large, but small area rugs scattered around soften the room and visually create a walkway.

END OF THE BED TRUNK
Worn paint and pretty patina decorate the long trunk that sits at the end of the bed. It provides seating and storage (a great place to store big blankets for chilly nights).

traditional motifs

Without question this masterful bedroom conjures up the coast with it's cabana stripes and naval blue, but it is given a modern spin in the way the elements have been layered.

GO CLASSIC
Patterns such as stripes, checks, and plaids never seem dated and create a clean simple look.

REFRESHING TWIST
Just because the prints are classics doesn't mean they have to be used in the traditional way. Rail-roaded fabric on the curtains, running the fabric horizontally instead of vertically, and mitering the stripes on the valance is a modern treatment.

WOOD, WOOD, WOOD
Classic beach homes are most always made of wood. In this master, walls and ceiling are given a coat of clean white paint for a fresh backdrop to the blue and white textiles. In other rooms the paneling was left natural for warmth and dimension.

DESIGNER TIP
The metal canopy is left unadorned to keep the room open and breezy.

DESIGNER TIP
Towels in the
bedroom are a
sure sign that
a pool or beach
is just beyond,
making it easy
to don your suit
and go.

DESIGNER TIP
Bring the outdoors indoors in more ways than one. This miniature palm has a bonsai feel and the outdoor metal chair is actually quite a comfy seat.

cloud nine

This milky wonder shows that white doesn't have to be boring. Splashes of gray blue make it feel warm and inviting.

ACCENT PILLOWS
The only pattern on the bedding comes from the coral print on the pillows. They stand out and dictate the coastal feel of the space.

SLIPCOVERED CHIC
The whole bed is slipcovered in white cotton duck, covering any contrasting wood or metal. With matching painted walls, the room feels sheathed in white.

BED BASKET
The pale blue basket at the foot of the bed holds white towels but also could be used for slippers or books and magazines.

RUG UNDERFOOT
The Oriental rug visually connects with the iron base on the bedside table and warms up the cool space.

Moroccan influence

Strong color is a focal point of Moroccan decorating, and the persimmon silk against the rich cobalt is right on cue. An intricately carved lamp and a stool with a woven seat transport you straight to Marrakech.

COBALT BLUE
A deep blue custom upholstered bed, from headboard to base, is covered in a durable ultrasuede fabric. The weight of the piece anchors the room.

VERMILLION AND WHITE
The vermillion accents almost border on an intense orange but are mediated by the creamy white in the gourd lamp, walls, window treatments, and bedside tables. The custom-trimmed duvet ties both colors together.

EXOTIC ELEMENTS
The curve of the headboard and the prints on the bed pillows all reference Middle Eastern motifs, which give the room an exotic flavor.

DESIGNER TIP
The contrast of the dark ceiling with the light walls makes the room feel cozy. Matching the curtains to the wall color makes them more function than feature.

DESIGNER TIP
Contrasting trim in shades of white against creamy walls adds interest.

neo-classic nest

This home is a lesson in classical architecture viewed through a playful, modern lens. Elements such as columns and trims are historically precise but executed with subtle, witty changes in materials or placement.

HISTORIC ELEMENTS

An Ionic column supports a cantilevered truss system on the expansive deck off this master bedroom, an unexpected combination with more modern materials.

VAULTED CEILING

Just right for breezy, beachy bedrooms, the expansive height of the room is matched by the windows, which let in ocean and sky.

SWEDISH SENSIBILITY

Swedish country style dictates the decor here. The pale bedside table and bench at the foot of the bed add soothing casualness to the space. To get the light, airy, European look, built-in nooks, and intricate moldings with planked wood siding done in pale shades were thoughtfully incorporated.

indulgent guest

Feminine and pretty, this guest room seems right out of a quaint bed & breakfast. Airy and light, it is a welcoming room that begs you to relax and stay awhile.

SHIPLAP WALLS
Rather than the traditional white painted shiplap, purple paint colors a feminine bedroom. The shade coordinates with the floral throw pillows on the bed and ties the room up in a neat little bow.

UPHOLSTERED HEADBOARD
A wood bed is upholstered with a green fabric that resembles grasscloth. The color brings in the pattern on the floral pillows and coordinates with the painted console table.

WINDOW TREATMENTS
Light streams through the windows but is diffused by simple, light curtains. They take the fussiness of the room down a peg but maintain the soft feel of the room.

"WE USED HEART PINE AND KEPT VISIBLE CRACKS BETWEEN THE BOARDS, THEN WE OMITTED STEPS IN THE REFINISHING PROCESS TO GET A WORN LOOK."

—HOMEOWNER

DESIGNER TIP
A demilune table's graceful legs mimic the lines of the chair. The bench at the end of the bed repeats the curvaceous theme.

DESIGNER TIP
A series of skylights bathes the room in light, keeping it bright when the sun is behind the hillside out the back door.

earth and sky

With nothing to see but the garden beyond and the clouds or stars above, this room boasts ultimate privacy and the feeling of a true escape from it all.

BASIC BED
Decorative pillows bridge the light and dark on this tailored bed upholstered in deep brown and dressed in white.

MIX IT UP
A sheer fabric drapes the upholstered bench at the end of the bed, a large scale pattern is used for the curtains, while prints and a smaller pattern are used as accents on the bed.

WALLS OF PANED GLASS
This unique wall brings architecture into the space and leads out to a private terrace situated at the base of hillside.

MATCHING CHESTS
The chests serve as bedside tables and storage.

DESIGNER TIP
A neutral-patterned rug keeps things soft underfoot and is stain resistant.

ELEMENTS OF STYLE

ORGANIC TEXTURES AND POPS OF BRIGHT COLOR LEND A BEACHY FEEL TO ANY BEDROOM.

tropical prints

Look for coastal motifs with large repeats for a modern twist that packs a punch.

rattan table

This scalloped edge adds a feminine touch to a classic piece.

beachy lighting

Lamps made of natural materials like driftwood give the room a carefree, just-washed-ashore vibe.

woven texture

From baskets to blinds to rugs to wallcoverings, woven textures lend a casual air to any space.

bold color

Go all in with a beachy-bright hue—just use it sparingly like on accent pillows and chairs.

coastal accessories

Bring the beach home with coastal-chic accessories like large shells or coral pieces.

tailored bedding

Piping or trim details give the room a crisp contrast to all the organic texture.

flexible furnishings

Choose pieces that can double as shoe-tying seating or tote bag storage.

DESIGNER TIP
Want the natural look without ponying up the dough for pricey grasscloth wallpaper? Opt for matchstick, bamboo, or woven shades instead!

DESIGNER TIP
For a beachy casual but super stylish look, hang drapes from a bamboo curtain rod installed as close to the ceiling as possible.

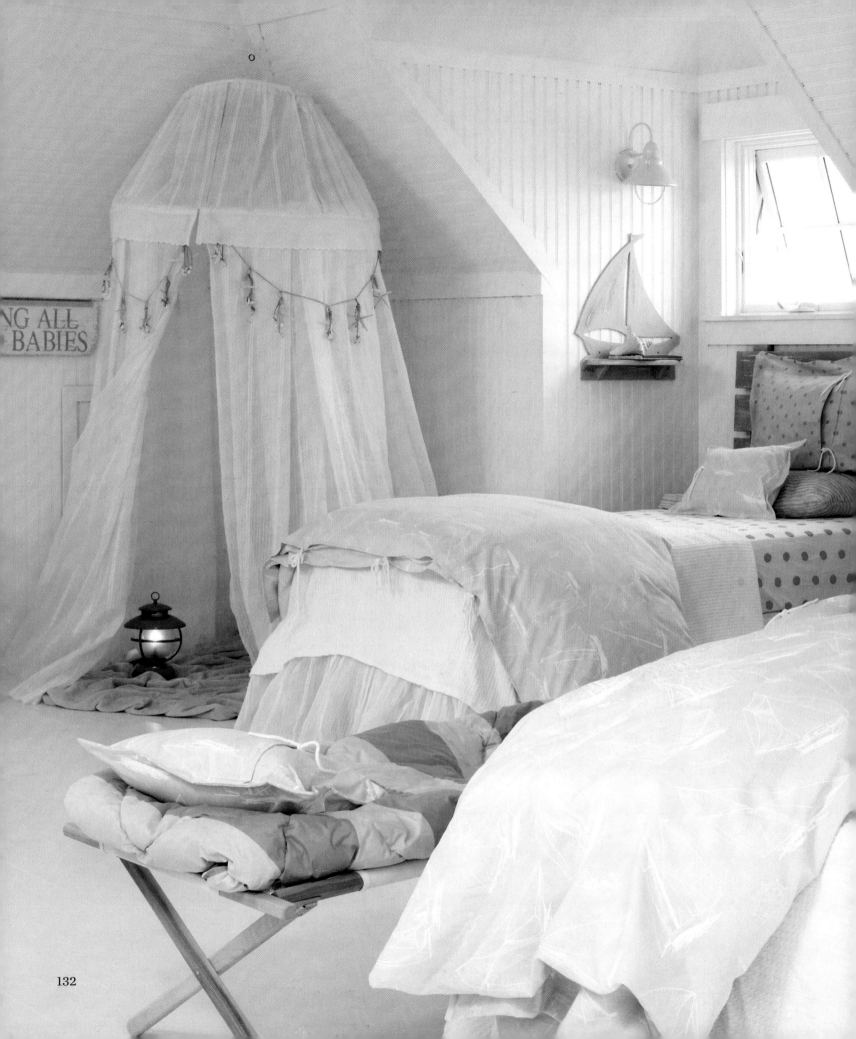

NG ALL BABIES

kids' rooms

Often the liveliest room in a beach house, kids' rooms reflect the fun and excitement of carefree vacations on the water. Bold color with lots of pattern takes center stage and is enhanced with vibrant art. Space-saving inventive built-ins create storage for beach gear, towels, and bathing suits. Bunk beds, double twin beds, and trundle beds are favorite choices to accommodate multiple siblings and friends, because more than anyplace else, the more-the-merrier concept rules at the beach.

ahoy there!

There's no question where passions lie in this house. Repeated nautical themes predominate and give the eye numerous places to rest. This room is a perfect escape for a pack of boys—and that's a lifesaver.

BARN DOOR
Enter the bunkroom through a sliding barn door with a cleat for a doorknob. A sliding door is a wonderful space-saving approach to privacy.

NAUTICAL BLUE EVERYWHERE
Once inside the room, blue is everywhere—in high gloss paint that makes the room glow with seaworthiness, in art on the walls, and in a soft cotton rug on the floor.

SHOTS OF RED AND WHITE
White custom-built beds are laid end to end. White sheets and red coverlets and pillows tie up the marine theme completely.

DESIGNER TIP
The painted striped floor is a fun nautical touch while the runner in the bedroom is a practical layer.

DESIGNER TIP
Tempering the dark wood
with shots of vivid color is
unexpected and very girly.

starry night

A small bedroom tucked in the eaves houses a built-in that accommodates two mattresses for sleeping in tandem and windows above for taking in the night sky.

GRANDMA'S ATTIC
What might be scary, with its dark walls and top of the house location, becomes an adventure with a pink palette. Part attic, part ship's cabin, this space seems conducive to imaginative escape.

GROSGRAIN
Strips of grosgrain ribbon provide the window treatments—a terrific idea if sunlight does not enter the room directly.

COLORFUL PILLOWS
The bedding is soft and light, so the beds come to life with sea star pillows and pink coverlets.

HIDDEN STORAGE
Built-in drawers that slide under the beds create functional storage for putting away clothes, toys or even extra bedding.

rock the casbah

Like a dreamy fun house full of whimsy, this bedroom setup is better than a storybook castle. Windows and crawl-throughs make late night stories a natural.

MAGIC CARPET
Patterned sheets and pillows and Morrocan details channel an exotic ride to dreamland.

PEEKABOO PASSAGEWAYS
The openings between the bunks repeat the shape of the niches and keep the whole look of the room consistent.

BUILT-IN LADDER
The ladder is affixed to the bunk, providing sure footing without the risk of it falling on anyone.

MOORISH DETAILS
The curvy cutouts and vivid colors were inspired by the original tilework found throughout the house.

DESIGNER TIP
Flushmount drawer hardware won't scrape shins and provides easy access to treasures stored inside.

DESIGNER TIP
Windows to the hall are framed deep enough to provide space for a book and can be closed for privacy.

"THE BEST ROOMS HAVE
A MIX OF WARM AND COOL
COLORS, AND KIDS ROOMS
AREN'T AN EXCEPTION.
THEY SHOULD BE FUN, YES,
BUT THEY'VE ALSO GOT TO BE
A PLACE TO GET AWAY TO
AND DREAM AND READ."

—PHILLIP SIDES, DESIGNER

primo bunks

This inventive use of space sleeps four comfortably, and its style appeals to adults and kids alike. Fitted coverlets mean bed-making is a cinch.

GIMME SHELTER
Four bunks built into customized private spaces are decorated with horizontal stripes that mimic the wood surround. It's a shipshape room with a place for everything to make tidying up as easy as possible.

CURTAINS
Pulled to enclose the space, curtains that cover the bunks from top to bottom block out light.

BUILT-IN CUBBIES
Nautical lanterns affixed to the top of the cubbies provide reading light. The nailhead design on the cubby doors adds a decorative element and a little character.

COLORS OF SUNDOWN
Earth tones fittingly collide with sunset hues suggesting evening has come.

sleepover setup

The dormer of this attic bedroom provides the perfect niche for an extra-guest setup. A camp cot is given loft with a cozy down comforter and equally soft blanket. Wire shelves provide a place to tuck clothes, bathing suits, and towels.

ROOM FOR MORE
Turn a tight spot or a nook in a child's room into a berth for pint-sized guests with the addition of an inexpensive canvas cot from the army surplus store.

CAMPING IN
Draped with sheets, this cot becomes the structure for an imaginative hideaway tent for hours of endless play.

BRIGHT AND LIGHT
Boys and girls are equally at home in rooms decorated in the colors of the sea. Mineral blues and chartreuse greens are happy colors for happy kids. Light bounces off white floors and painted walls.

DESIGNER TIP
Replace or restore windows in older homes so that they are fully functional to allow breezes in.

ELEMENTS OF STYLE

COMBINE BOLD COLOR, CHEERY PRINTS, AND WHIMSICAL ACCESSORIES FOR A CHIC KIDS' RETREAT.

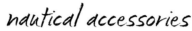

bright accents

Paint picture frames, chairs, or table a bold color to add energy in kids' bedroom or play space.

nautical accessories

Create a beach escape with classically coastal accents like pillows made of sail flags [or porthole-like windows].

durable furnishings

Outfit a kids' room with pieces like this molded fiberglass rocker that [are easy to move and] can take a lot of wear and tear.

a worldly touch

Globes and maps not only add bright color but also inspire dreams of far-flung travels.

plush coverlets and throws

Soften the space with quilts and blankets in colors that hide dirt and materials that can be washed.

playful decor

No kids' room would be complete without a touch of whimsy, like these shell-encrusted initials.

cheerful prints

Instill an upbeat mood with patterned fabrics in beachy hues like sunshine yellow and turquoise blue.

DESIGNER TIP
Elevated, built-in bunks create extra storage space like drawers and cubbies. Add partial walls that work as headboards and give each sleeper a little privacy.

DESIGNER TIP
Frame an opening in divider walls with vintage porthole windows – they up the fun factor and add coastal charm.

porches

The beach is all about indoor-outdoor living. As an extension of the home, porches offer alfresco opportunities for many activities—dining, sleeping, relaxing, reading, and reconnecting. Whether you have a small urban deck or several thousand square feet in the suburbs, adopting a few of the inspired ideas on the pages that follow will lend a coastal vibe to your outdoor oasis.

best of the old

Chartreuse Greek key patterned upholstery, rattan chairs, wood fans, a beaded-board ceiling, and large palm plants all contribute to the feeling of retro style. Furniture, formal and informal, wearing a universal coat of white paint adds to the impression.

RUN LONG

A porch that extends the length of the house's beachfront side provides space for multiple seating areas. Color and patterned upholstery is a way to delineate each area.

FLOORS AND CEILINGS

Painted floors and white ceilings help keep the space cool and reflect light rather than absorb it. A quality porch paint or a high-gloss lacquer is a good choice.

LAMP LIGHT

No pendant or overhead lights, but lamps scattered throughout the porch focus illumination on an area and provide task lighting for those sitting outside at night. The lack of overhead lights prevents harsh light that might make the room unwelcoming when it is dark outside.

AWNINGS DESCEND

Glassed-in porches mean you can sit outside no matter the weather, but they also bake in the hottest times of the day. Awnings descend to shade intense light as the day heats up.

COLOR AND PATTERN

Lots of trees outside dapple sunlight on the porch, and the greenery reaches inside with the plants and green upholstery.

DESIGNER TIP Awnings descend to block out intense light and keep the room comfortable.

DESIGNER TIP
For an unobstructed view, think beyond the usual railing materials. Wire, or even plexiglass, is a great choice.

Caribbean cool

The tones of the wood, water, and foliage take center stage, making any additional colors unnecessary. It is understandable why the porch is the gathering place here. A deep roof provides protection from the elements so you can always take in the view.

ALL WOOD
Classic West Indies Teak furniture withstands the beating sun and driving monsoon rains and comes out all the better as it softly grays overtime to match the stained deck.

FENCE RAILS
Rather than vertical or horizontal pickets, wire runs horizontally to preserve the view of the water as much as possible. It protects those on the porch, but doesn't impede the view.

DAPPLED SHADE
Because of the cooling breezes in the Caribbean, shade need not be all encompassing. Dappled light and a moveable overhang help direct shade.

suite of teak

There is something very ordered in a collection of teak furniture with similar lines. It's a material that works well in the humid South, and the designs these days look just as good inside the house as out.

GEOMETRY LESSONS

The custom pillows borrow their colors from the environment and mirror the ceiling's crossbeams. Adding to the play is the striped outdoor rug laid across the lines of the deck. A round coffee table and cylindrical ceramic garden seats are nice counterpoints to all the lines and angles.

PLANTS INSIDE AND OUT

The palm trees blowing in the wind and the potted palms on the porch blur the lines between beach and home.

DESIGNER TIP
Carved brackets add loads of architectural interest to the slender porch posts.

DESIGNER TIP
The deep ledge is a perfect spot for accessories or can serve as extra seating.

154

woodland escape

Wide porch columns sheathed in the same cedar shakes as the house create window-like openings for taking in the lush view. After a day of sailing or crabbing, this is the place to kick back.

ALL WICKER
The sofa, chairs, and footstools are all wicker, which flies in the face of prevailing wisdom to use different materials to make a space more interesting. But the shingles introduce another wood, and the fabric is varied throughout the arrangement.

LANTERN SCONCES
Simple and unassuming and just restrained enough to work with the arrangement on the porch, sconces flank both sets of French doors to give light on the porch and illuminate it so it can be enjoyed from inside too.

GREAT VIEWS
Whether the view beyond is lush and green or rolling waves and sandy shore, keep contrasts and collections minimal. It is impossible to compete with the action beyond the porch.

tropical paradise

Dense rainforestlike surroundings cocoon this pleasant escape. Comfortable furnishings with thick cushions and plump throw pillows make it an outdoor "room" in the truest sense.

SATURATED SHADES
Green painted columns reflect the foliage all around the porch and connect to it visually.

FLOWER POWER PINK
Hot pink accent pillows and cushions echo the flowers beyond the porch.

TILED FLOOR
Terra-cotta tiles extend into the house, providing a seamless transition from indoors to outdoors.

DARK WOOD
Dark wood, ornate carved chairs and sofa bring a weight to the space and make the porch feel even more like a living room.

DESIGNER TIP
Dark green and white is a classic color combination, but the punches of fuschia give this porch an island edge.

DESIGNER TIP
A pale blue on the ceiling provides cool contrast and keeps bugs at bay.

colonial gem

With all the trimmings of colonial style, this home has a welcoming graciousness about it. Ample seating suggests this is a well-used porch. Little touches like the potted cleome and vase of flowers are green accents that fit the scheme.

RATTAN CLUB CHAIRS
Painted black, the rattan chairs and patterned cushions are the stars of the space. The flecking paint shows their age, but the outdoor fabric gives them a fresh look.

PAINTED WHITE
The crisp railing and the chairs and bench provide a clean contrast with the worn wood floor and aged rattan chairs.

CARPET OF GREEN
The outdoor rug connects visually with the grass and brings another element of color and life onto the porch.

SHIP'S LANTERN
The overhead lantern and matching sconce suit the location of the house in Maine and illuminate the arrangement below.

ELEMENTS OF STYLE

CREATE A SIT-DOWN, STAY-A-WHILE OUTDOOR LIVING ROOM WITH COMFORTABLE FURNISHINGS THAT STAND UP TO THE ELEMENTS WITHOUT SACRIFICING GOOD LOOKS.

all-weather furnishings
Teak bases and water-and-fade-resistant upholstery are great choices for withstanding intense sunshine and coastal mist.

colorful lanterns
Either wired or candle-lit, these lanterns set a romantic tone and add a cheerful pop of color.

acrylic servingware
Keep the space party-ready with hard-to-break serving pieces like this acrylic set.

sculptural chairs
Just because they're meant for outdoor use doesn't mean they can't have style. Opt for pieces with detailed backs and legs to give your porch some panache.

extra seating
Try a garden stool or a small ottoman for easy-to-move seating to accommodate a crowd.

beachy accessories
Planters, like this nautilus shell-shaped one, and other accent pieces, like a shell-encrusted mirror, lend a vacation vibe to any porch.

natural materials
Connect the space to the surrounding scenery with accessories made of natural materials, like this cork bar set or woven trays, chargers, or coasters.

DESIGNER TIP
Soften a bench, settee, or hammock with punchy pillows made from weather-resistant fabrics.

DESIGNER TIP
High-gloss white aluminum chairs withstand the elements and would be equally welcome indoors.

MAKE-OVERS
BEFORE & AFTERS

Home makeovers don't always require major construction or financial investment. Often a coat of paint or an infusion of accessories takes a space from dated to dazzling. Making more involved modifications like adding efficient windows or enlarging kitchens and baths can elevate both comfort and style. And when a major overhaul is necessary, detailed planning and design is the key to creating a home that stands the test of time.

exterior

A top priority was safeguarding the 680-square-foot tent-shaped plywood structure on the Gulf of Mexico. Fresh coats of paint and stain helped stabilize and protect the wood exterior. The cement board siding and a peeling deck, where the homeowners spend most of their time, were coated with solid acrylic stain.

easy updates to

bring back a bungalow

The modern lines of a 1960s
Florida kit house are revealed after a
budget-friendly makeover

THE PROBLEM: Mostly age and neglect. Salt air was taking a toll on the exterior. Over the years, chairs and other objects filled up the house, defeating the purpose of its modern, streamlined design.

THE SOLUTION: The home reflects its original intent—clean and spare, open to the sea and air, with great views, indulgent textures, and a true escape from the clutter and distraction of everyday life.

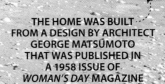

THE HOME WAS BUILT
FROM A DESIGN BY ARCHITECT
GEORGE MATSUMOTO
THAT WAS PUBLISHED IN
A 1958 ISSUE OF
WOMAN'S DAY MAGAZINE

165

living room

Every surface was stripped of its covering. Original plywood walls were stained a semi-transparent version of the exterior stain. Floors, ceilings, and glass windows were returned to better-than-original glory. Inexpensive furnishings and natural fabrics and textiles keep things airy and fresh.

project details

WHAT THEY KEPT: All of the kit house's original plywood walls, floors, ceilings, and glass windows.

WHAT THEY SALVAGED: The original fireplace got a face-lift, so it's more in keeping with the overall design of the house. And a left-behind daybed that was destined for the dump became a super-comfy sofa (above), with a new mattress, cushions, and custom pillows in cotton and linen.

WHAT THEY SCRAPPED: A worn-out carpet, extra furniture, old mattresses, damp-rotted cabinetry, chipped yellow laminate countertops, old appliances, original linoleum, cheap wood paneling, the cabinet over the island, and a bunch of bulky bar chairs.

BEFORE

BEFORE

kitchen

As in the rest of the house, the scheme here stays subdued and monochromatic, and the windows are left bare in deference to the view beyond. A freestanding, white enamel fireplace makes a modern statement and warms the open home on blustery days.

we love...

POPS OF WHITE. From satiny enamel paint on the plywood floors and stove to the crisp finish of the appliances and countertops, white pairs beautifully with the sandy-hued woodwork.

THE REFRIGERATOR NICHE. The front of the house is one great room, so the refrigerator would be easily seen were it not for a niche that was built to encase and thus conceal the lines of the appliance.

the quick list

THEN	NOW
Carpet-covered cottage	Painted white floors
Bad paneling	Painted plywood walls
Peeling deck and siding	Exterior covered with acrylic stain to protect it from the elements
Dark, wood-tone space	Light, airy, modern rooms

easy ways to
let the sunshine in

A drab 1970s house on a Santa Barbara beach perks
up with minimal interiors and gallons of white paint

THE PROBLEM:

Homes on the California coast rarely come up for sale, so despite its dated look, the owners felt lucky when this two-story architectural mishmash came on the market. Inside, gray dominated, from paint to linoleum to dark tinted windows. Outside, pavement stretched all the way to the back door.

THE SOLUTION:

The owner had the builder make everything white. With the darkness lifted, the soaring ceilings and incredible views immediately took center stage and inspired a new, light, airy decor.

we love...

AN OASIS OUT THE DOOR. It's nice to have a green buffer between the sea and sand and the house. Plants add life to the expansive deck and serve as a windbreak.

STRIPES! The home's linear design is echoed in the rugs, fabrics, and sleek furnishings.

BEFORE

sitting room

Built-in seating and a custom-lacquered coffee table provide a comfy nook for taking in views from the second floor. Coral, sand, and nautical stripes—are subtle nods to the beach.

BEFORE

best tricks for
bringing back the charm

Dilapidated and neglected, a house on Tybee Island finds its true soul with an unpretentious approach that reveals a veneration for the past

BEFORE

THE PROBLEM Built in 1904, the house leaned a little to the right, had aluminum windows, cheap paneling, wall-to-wall carpet, and acoustical-tile ceilings.

THE SOLUTION After stripping away layers of convenience that denatured the original house, the homeowners added insulation, heating, and air conditioning, and updated the kitchen and bath. The final product is not state-of-the-art, but feels and looks its age and will comfortably shelter another generation of families at the beach.

BEFORE

A SCREENED DOOR.
Victorian details come to
life on an exterior door
painted robin's egg blue
and used to to camouflage
the pantry's contents.

174

living area

For the open kitchen/dining/living spaces, the answer was white—on the furniture, lamp shades, appliances, and every inch of the walls and ceilings.

5 things to look for in a home worth saving

1. ORIGINAL WINDOWS They are the heart of the house. "If they're too rotten to salvage or local codes don't permit, keep the authentic sashes and reuse them inside," says Jane Coslick, designer.

2. OLD WOOD "Look for original wood beneath carpet and behind drywall or cheap paneling. Wood gives a house its character."

3. LOCATION "Make sure there will be value in the property after the restoration is complete."

4. STRUCTURAL SOUNDNESS Hire a professional to inspect the big-ticket items. Get an estimate on bringing plumbing, wiring, and HVAC up to code. Always have the home checked for termites. "Make sure it isn't beyond repair."

5. HISTORY WORTH HONORING "I look for old photos and talk with the neighbors to find out what the house originally looked like," Jane says.

we love...
RUSTIC BOARDS,
Wood in the original
house was repurposed
in the dressing area of
the new home, covering
walls adjacent to the
outdoor shower.

BEFORE

the quick list

THEN	NOW
Sagging house with no air-conditioning	Rustic, breezy weekend getaway
Unlevel wraparound porch	Enclosed new master bedroom
Wall-to-wall carpet	Bare wood floors, some painted
Bad vintage kitchen with sad laminate wood cabinets	Chic, shiplap-clad kitchen with glass-tile countertops
Frumpy upholstered furniture	White slipcovers that make everything look new

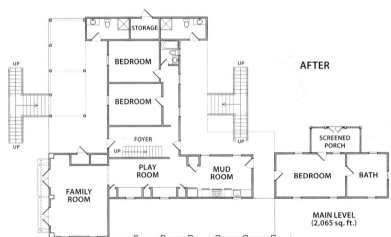

UP

UP

STORAGE

BEDROOM

BEDROOM

UP

UP

AFTER

FOYER

SCREENED PORCH

PLAY ROOM

MUD ROOM

BEDROOM

BATH

FAMILY ROOM

MAIN LEVEL (2,065 sq. ft.)

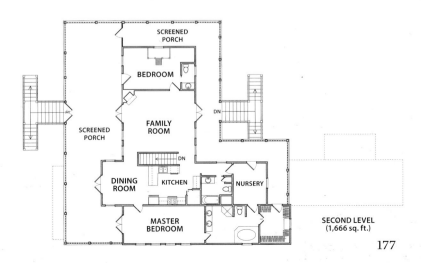

SCREENED PORCH

BEDROOM

DN

SCREENED PORCH

FAMILY ROOM

DN

DINING ROOM

KITCHEN

NURSERY

MASTER BEDROOM

SECOND LEVEL (1,666 sq. ft.)

177

a savvy plan to
max out a small house

A decrepit house in Manhattan Beach
with a rental past becomes a quaint
cottage that reflects its 1920s origins

we love...
VIVID FABRICS
Bold patterns mixed
with stripes and
graphic prints keep
things eclectic.

THE PROBLEM The bungalow had all of the signatures
of a 1970s beach shack with none of the retro cool.

THE SOLUTION Cedar-shake shingles now clad the
new bungalow that has grown from one bedroom
to four while maintaining its original footprint. New
pitched ceilings and skylights add more light to the
space while light hardwood floors give the house a
sense of age and keep the mood airy.

living room

THE FIRST STEP: A coat of pale paint to brighten the space, which was the original storage shed, followed by the addition of a deck to expand the living area outdoors and take in the view.

BEFORE

we love...
ACCESSORIES REMINISCENT OF THE BEACH Elements like the capiz shell pendant light and kitchen accessories in shades of sea and sunshine.

BEFORE

kitchen

Wainscot gives the space a more established look, and a picture ledge hangs below the ceiling, which is covered in V-groove paneling. Extra-thick countertops were a splurge, but well worth it for their sense of style and character.

decorating at the beach

PALETTE Allover white with accents of greens and blues.

PATTERN Mix them but balance large and small scale prints for a unified effect.

UPHOLSTERY Upholstered pieces should have clean modern lines, and then you can mix things up with vintage and eclectic pieces.

STATEMENT PIECES Seek out statement pieces that will personalize the space. They can be quirky or just bold colored, but they should be something that will stay in your memory and that of your guests.

BEFORE

we love...

HITS OF YELLOW. Paired with gray-blue tones, it's a marriage with modern flair. ORGANIC MOTIFS. The medallion embroidery on the bedding and the framed coral prints on the wall conjure up botanicals, bringing the outside in.

we love...

CHIPPENDALE CHAIRS
They're timeless, graphic classics that work equally well in traditional and contemporary settings.
COMPOSITIONS. On tabletops or walls, an artful arrangement of accessories adds interest and draws the eye to explore.

THE 1920s HOUSE NEEDED TO LOOK ITS AGE—
NOT LIKE THE 1970s HALFWAY HOUSE IT RESEMBLED

BEFORE

AFTER

BEFORE

OUTDOOR SHED	DECK
	LIVING ROOM
OFFICE	DINING ROOM
LIVING ROOM	KITCHEN
	BEDROOM
KITCHEN	W/D
GARAGE	BEDROOM CARPORT
ENTRY	
MAIN LEVEL (1,226 SQ. FT.)	**MAIN LEVEL** (1,529 SQ. FT.)

the quick list

THEN	NOW
One-bedroom shack	Four-bedroom bungalow
Painted white-brick house	Cedar-shake exterior
A nothing-special entrance surrounded by a sea of concrete brick	Entrance tucked into the side of the house with curb appeal-boosting pavers leading up to it
Drab, wood-finished interior	White painted rooms throughout
Claustrophobia-inducing low windows	Pitched ceilings with skylights

lessons learned from
a total transformation

A Maine eyesore might have been torn down. Instead, it was lovingly restored so that it's now a source of pride for the homeowners and neighbors

BEFORE

THE PROBLEM Situated near the water, the house was a relic of the 1960s ranch style. It needed updating, an expansion, and a face-lift to make it appropriate to the setting.

THE SOLUTION The transformation made the home age and style appropriate with exposed beams, shutters, and wood interiors. The architect preserved the central structure, adding two wings with three rooflines at different angles. A porch faces the water on one side of the house, and on the other a broad deck offers room for lounging. A two-story fieldstone fireplace anchors the new great room.

exterior

At 2,200 square feet, the former ranch is deceptively large. It looks like it is only one and a half stories from the street entrance, while its full two-and-a-half-story height is visible from the water.

we love...

FUNCTIONING SHUTTERS
Not mere decorative treatments, though they are carved with abstract sailboats, the shutters can be closed in the event of harsh winds and inclement weather.

187

kitchen

Rough-sawn local pine dresses the house, while the kitchen's floors are made from teak and holly, woods that are often used on yachts.

we love...

STAINED WOOD walls, ceilings, and floors that create a seamless backdrop.

project details

WHAT THEY KEPT: Just the spectacular view.

WHAT THEY SALVAGED: The architect preserved the central structure and added two wings with three rooflines, all at different angles.

WHAT THEY SCRAPPED: The ranch-style layout and color of the original house, and also the original materials—such as the flooring, walls, and roof.

189

we love...

THE TWO-STORY
FIELDSTONE FIREPLACE
Made from local stones,
it creates a stunning
focal point in the living
room and complements
the white pine frame
and trusses.

190

BEFORE

10 tips for historic renovation

1. CHOOSE a contractor who expresses a love of and knowledge of old houses. It is much more important than the lowest bid.

2. RESEARCH your house and those like it, so you know as much as possible before you get started.

3. STAY TRUE to your house so that you have the cottage you fell in love with and not something that feels new and unfamiliar.

4. PRESERVE as much of the original as possible. It may be more expensive, but once you remove its historic character, it's impossible to retrieve.

5. START SEARCHING EARLY for things like light fixtures and doorknobs, paint colors, and other hardware so that you are using what you want, not just what will make do.

6. BUY THE BEST that you can afford, and make choices to save on some things so you can splurge on others. It is worth it now, and you will be grateful later if you buy the best quality when there is a choice.

7. BE WILLING TO CHANGE your mind or have it changed. Sometimes better options present themselves, and being open to them makes for a better result.

8. DON'T LET the professionals you hire intimidate you. Most shortcuts lead to disappointment.

9. AVOID TRENDS AND FADS. Stick with the classics and you'll be glad two years down the road.

10. BE PATIENT. Life happens. It's worth the wait to get it right.

COLOR GUIDE

Perhaps more than any other element of a room's decor, it is color that sets the tone. Whether light and airy, rich and cocooning, bright and energetic, the color choices for walls, trim, and even furniture can yield the greatest impact for the smallest cost. On the pages that follow, you will find swatches that represent the predominant colors of the coastal regions featured in this book.

Mainsail White—An off-white that doesn't feel stark or cold and yet works well with shades of blue.

NEW ENGLAND

This region boasts a more traditional palette for exteriors like gray, gray-blue, and taupe. Weathered shades are punched up with accents in navy blue and cranberry, often in shiny lacquer finishes. Think nautical chic.

Summer Sea—Inspired by the petals of a hydrangea bush and the water in July, this blue works well with other blues and the occasional wild card color.

Sailor Red—Definitely to be used in moderation, lest the whole red, white, and blue palette take over. This bold shade shakes up the blue and white formula that can sometimes be too predictable.

Night Sky—This is a navy blue that might show up in mattress ticking or trim or other nautical icons around the house. It can also be dramatic if it's used in large areas.

Scoop of Vanilla—A soft white with a hint of yellow in it, it soaks up the sun streaming through Southern windows.

the SOUTH

From the crisp white of antebellum houses with deep green-black shutters to bright sorbet accents as you move further southward, the colors of the South span the spectrum.

Aqua Pool—An intense color, it is best used in small doses on pillows and accent furniture.

Lime Sherbet—Lilly Pulitzer colors have come into the house and now brighten up sun-drenched spaces.

Strawberry Shake—Pink is a flattering color, and Southern women will find a way to get a little into the house.

KEY WEST

The colors here are as unique as the residents—bright, unexpected, with an eye to the artistic. No color is off-limits, but shades of citrus yellow and green with hints of melon and hibiscus are commonplace.

Verdant White—With just the subtlest hint of green, the color looks at home in a space surrounded by lush flora.

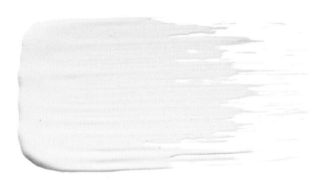

Smiley Face—The opaque yellow evokes intensely-colored citrus fruit and would be best in small doses and as an accent color.

Retro Green—A little minty and a little preppy, the color will coordinate with the vegetation but also fight for its own turf.

Flamingo Red—With a hint of pink in its pigment, the color also works well as an accent, heating up a space or bringing a little more intensity to it.

Sand Dollar—Stucco walls, mosquito nets, and white cotton duck slipcovers and coverlets all love this shade.

the CARIBBEAN

Sun-bleached stucco, indigenous wood tones, and contrasting colors (such as the teal blues and greens of varying ocean depths and the brick and corals of the terra-cotta tile roofs) exemplify Caribbean style.

Clay Roof—Terra-cotta colors appear in prints and patterns, but they are most frequently visible as building materials, bringing a warmth and texture to every space.

Lagoon—Limpid blue with a little West Indies turquoise thrown in, we see this as upholstery and the color of accessories.

Deep Blue Sea—A saturated shade that reflects the color of the ocean as it deepens.

Hollywood Sign—A soft white that gets crisper or creamier depending on the light.

SOUTHERN CALIFORNIA

Southern California is about sand, sea, and golden light with a bit of sequoia and redwood thrown in. It is expressed through an earthy palette with colors that can work as both neutral base and edgy accents.

Malibu Blue—The blue matches the water and the seaglass that collectors bring in from the beach and use as inspiration around their houses. It should be used as a small accent.

Golden State—This earthy shade of yellow reflects the natural and organic leanings of the Southern California aesthetic.

Sequoia Bark—In small doses, deep brown serves as an accent color on trim. It seems inspired by woods and the earth.

Cappuccino Froth—A creamy white that works with the dusted down colors of the region.

the PACIFIC NORTHWEST

Rustic, raw, and natural, the untamed landscape of the Pacific Northwest dictates the hues that figure into its architecture—fir green and story ocean grounded by the color of coffee and earth.

Mushroom Compost—A rich milk-chocolate brown recalls faded shingles and tree bark.

Moss Rock—Reminiscent of dried out lichen on rocks, this green comes off neutral.

After-the-Rain Blue—Like a late-afternoon, fog-tinged sky, this blue goes traditional with cream or modern with the other colors in the palette.

living room

measurements:

square footage: .... (length x width)

style cues:

....
....
....
....
....

my wish list:

....
....
....
....
....
....

other notes:

....
....
....

color swatches: (attach here)

dining space

measurements:

square footage: .... (length x width)

style cues:

....
....
....
....
....

my wish list:

....
....
....
....
....
....

other notes:

....
....
....

color swatches: (attach here)

kitchen

measurements:

square footage: **(length x width)**

style cues:

my wish list:

other notes:

color swatches: (attach here)

bathroom

measurements:

square footage: **(length x width)**

style cues:

my wish list:

other notes:

color swatches: (attach here)

master bedroom

measurements:

square footage: (length x width)

style cues:

my wish list:

other notes:

color swatches: (attach here)

guest bedroom

measurements:

square footage: (length x width)

style cues:

my wish list:

other notes:

color swatches: (attach here)

kids' bedroom

measurements:

square footage: **(length x width)**

style cues:

my wish list:

other notes:

color swatches: (attach here)

porch

measurements:

square footage: **(length x width)**

style cues:

my wish list:

other notes:

color swatches: (attach here)

paint finish guide

PAINT TYPES:

LATEX:
Water-based and best for most jobs. It dries quickly and provides easy cleanup.

OIL-BASED:
Hard, durable finish for wood and moist environments like exteriors, kitchens and baths.

PAINT FINISHES:

FLAT FINISH:
A matte finish that is ideal for masking surface imperfections.

EGGSHELL FINISH:
A barely perceptible sheen that is easier to clean than flat finish paint.

SATIN OR PEARL FINISH:
Glossier than eggshell finish that is both durable and washable.

SEMI-GLOSS FINISH:
Noticeable sheen highlights trim beautifully and is good for damp bathrooms and kitchens

HIGH-GLOSS:
The shiniest finish, used to showcase trim, cabinets, floors or furniture. It is very durable and washable.

resources

LIVING ROOM
page 62

LAMP: Crackle Gourd Glass Lamp, $349, Cottage & Bungalow; 877/441-9222 or cottageandbungalow.com

TABLE: *Coastal Living* Beachcomber table in Sea Mist, Stanley Furniture; 276/627-2540 or stanleyfurniture.com for prices and retailers

RUG: Aquinnah cotton woven rug, $28–$385 depending on size, Dash & Albert Rug Company; 800/658-5035 or dashandalbert.com

FABRIC (bottom to top): Odyssey Quest, No. 9 Thompson; Khiva, Jim Thompson; Ottomania Izmir, No. 9 Thompson; jimthompsonfabrics.com

PILLOWS: Pillows, $120–$295; Waterleaf Interiors, 310/545-3175 or waterleafinteriors.com

VASE: Large Textured Vase, $450; 828/275-8279 or elementclaystudio.com

DINING ROOM
page 80

SIDEBOARD: *Coastal Living* Seaside Inn sideboard in Morning Sky, Stanley Furniture; 276/627-2540 or stanleyfurniture.com for prices and retailers

CORAL BOWL: Coral Branch Decorative Bowls, $92 for two, Two's Company; 866/421-1744 or madisonavegifts.com

NAPKIN RINGS: Antique Silver Napkin Rings, $32 for set of six; 888/779-5176 or potterybarn.com

DISHES: Lotus dessert plate, $8, and bowl, $4; 800/309-2500 or anthropologie.com

CANDLESTICKS: Antique silver candle-holders, $24 each, and vintage urn with lid, $105; 800/896-7266 or twoscompany.com for retailers

FABRIC: Minos in Aquatics; raoul textiles.com for showrooms; Seeds in Sky, available to the trade, Galbraith & Paul; 215/508-0800 or galbraithandpaul.com for showrooms

CHAIR: Green Bentwood Chair, $150; 866/755-9079 or conranusa.com

KITCHEN
page 96

LIGHT FIXTURE: Union pendant in Polished Nickel with shade in Modern Aqua, $171, Schoolhouse Electric, 800/630-7113 or schoolhouseelectric.com

FRIDGE: Beach Cruiser Series refrigerator, starting at $3,295, Big Chill; 877/842-3269 or bigchillfridge.com

STOOL: Malibu Channeled diner stool, $186, American Chairs; 888/831-7629 or americanchairs.com

GLASSES: Sea Glass Goblet and Tumbler, $12–$14, Anthropologie; 800/309-2500 or anthropologie.com

METAL BUCKET: Silver & Rope Barware Bowl, $275, Pieces; 404/869-2476 or piecesinc.com

DISHES: Fiestaware Dinner Plate in Turquoise, $17, Salad Plate in Sunflower, $11, and Mug in Tangerine, $13, Macy's; 800/289-6229 or macys.com

BATHROOM
page 110

TOWELS: Silver Resin Whelk Shell, $28, Lazy Susan; 888/578-7288 or lazysusanusa.com; Auberge Bath Towels, $9 to $34, Matouk; matouk.com for retailers

MIRROR: Oyster Shell Mirror, Square, $310, Currey & Company; 877/768-6428 or curreycodealers.com for showrooms

KNOBS: Cabinet hardware from Rejuvenation; 888/401-1900 or rejuvenation.com

FAUCET: Classic Bridge faucet from Rohl; 800/777-9762 or rohlhome.com

LIGHT FIXTURE: Industrial-style pendant lamps by Visual Comfort, available through Circa Lighting; 877/762-2323 or circalighting.com

SOAP: Saltwater Soap with Rosemary and Patchouli, $8 each; 718/624-2929 or saipua.com

TILE: iridescent glass from Oceanside Glasstile; glasstile.com for dealers

BEDROOM
page 130

PILLOW: Green Monstera Leaf pillow, $16.95, Pier 1 Imports; 800/245-4595 or pier1.com for retailers

SHEETS: Rope Percale Bedding, $58 to $378, Williams-Sonoma Home; 888/922-4108 or wshome.com

BENCH: Made Goods Nico Large Bench in Beige; 631/287-5015 or mecoxgardens.com

LAMP: Driftwood Lamp Base in Natural Beige (shade not included), $420; alldriftwoodfurniture.com

CHAIR: Bungalow 5 Audrey chair, $550, Revival Home & Garden; 206/763-3886 or revivalhomeandgarden.com

WALLCOVERING: Cotton Grass Wallcovering, $24.50 per roll; creativewallcovering.com

TABLE: Palm Beach Scalloped Bamboo End Table, $1,161; laneventure.com for retailers

SHELL PAPERWEIGHT: Silver Resin Whelk Shell, $28, Lazy Susan; 888/578-7288 or lazysusanusa.com

KIDS' ROOM
page 144

GLOBE: Cram's Project Globe (16-inch), Murray Hudson; 800/748-9946 or murrayhudson.com for pricing and purchase info.

ROCKING CHAIR: Fiberglass Shell Rocker Side Chair in Ocean, $285, Modernica; modernica.net

FABRIC: Star Burst in East, Peter Dunham Textiles; peterdunham.com for showrooms; Casablanca in Sky/Mustard and Tangier in Tangelo/Natural, Kathryn Ireland; kathrynireland.com for showrooms.

THROW: Pom Pom Throw in Turquoise, $98, Viva Terra; 800/233-6011 or vivaterra.com

PILLOWS: Handmade pure-linen pillows in St. Barts, $65 each; 415/577-8589 or coastal-cushions.com

LETTERS: Small Alphabet Letters, $35 each; pattisartfuldesign.com

OUTDOOR SPACE
page 160

CHAIR: Day Lily II armchair in White Lite with seat cushion in Pacific, from $1,475, Brown Jordan; 800/743-4252 or brownjordan.com

GLASSES: Acrylic drinkware in Blue, $4.25 to $19.95, Pier 1 Imports; 800/245-4595 or pier1.com for retailers

LOUNGE CHAIR: Starck Robinwood Deluxe chaise, Sutherland; 800/717-8325 or sutherlandfurniture.com for prices and retailers

STOOL: Desi stool in Canary Yellow, $535, Shine Home; 800/574-4634 or shopshinehome.com

PLANTER: Two's Company Large Nautilus Shell Vase, $180, Madison Ave Gifts; 866/421-1744 or madisonavegifts.com

ICE BUCKET: Gold Cork Ice Bucket & Tongs, $195, Kim Seybert; 631/329-6200 or kimseybert.com for retailers

LANTERNS: Square Green Lanterns, $10–$30; 800/245-4595 or pier1.com

index

photography credit

Jean Allsopp: 16, 17, 20, 24, 25 right, 27, 63, 64, 74, 120, 132, 134, 142, 148, 152, 156; **Steven Brooke:** 26 top; **Troy Campbell:** 26 bottom, 88, 164, 166, 167, 168, 169; **Brian Carter:** 32 bottom; **Grey Crawford:** 178, 179, 180, 181 top, 181 bottom, 182, 184, 185; **Roger Davies:** 14, 21 top left, 36 left, 38 bottom right, 39, 44, 76, 92, 98, 128; **Erica George Dines:** 111; **Colleen Duffley:** 18 left, 21 top right, 136; **Josh Savage Gibson:** 32 top right, 106, 131, 146; **Tria Giovan:** 13, 15 top right, 15 bottom left, 52, 54 lead, 54 inset, 56, 60, 70, 86, 102, 103, 108, 118, 140, 158; **Dan Heringa:** 42 left, 43, 45 top, 45 bottom; **Mike Jensen:** 94; **Richard Leo Johnson:** 19, 81, 84, 172, 174, 175 top, 175 bottom, 176, 177; **Deborah Whitlaw Llewellyn:** 15 bottom right, 31 right, 32 top left, 37, 50, 58, 68, 82, 90, 97, 112, 114, 127, 145, 150; **Robert Mauer:** 22, 23; **Jeff McNamara:** 104; **Tom McWilliam:** 116; **Shelly Metcalf:** 38 bottom left; **Keith Scott Morton:** 12; **Laura Moss:** 122, 138; **Lisa Romerein:** 34, 35, 38 top, 72, 170, 171; **Claudio Santini:** 40, 41; **Thomas Storey:** 100; **Tim Street-Porter:** 10, 11, 15 top left; **Jonny Valiant:** 21 bottom, 125, 154, 161; **Brian Vanden Brink:** 28, 29, 30, 48, 66, 78, 187, 188, 189, 190, 191; **Dominique Vorillon:** 33